Comfort Soups

30 Healthy and Nutritious Recipes

of Authentic, Vegetarian and Farmhouse Soups

Copyright Notice

Reproduction, duplication, transmission of this document in part or in whole is permitted only with written permission from the publisher. All rights reserved.

Respective brands and trademarks mentioned in this book belong to their respective owners.

Disclaimer

This document is geared towards providing summarization of information related to the topic. While all attempts have been made to verify the accuracy of the information, the author does not assume any responsibility for errors, omissions, or interpretations of the content. The information is offered for informational or entertainment purposes only. If professional advice is necessary, a qualified legal, medical, financial or another respective professional should be consulted. **The reader is responsible for his or her own actions. The publisher does not accept any responsibility or liability arising from damages or losses, real or perceived, direct or indirect, resulting from the use of this information.**

Table of Contents

Foreword 8
Chapter One: Why You Should Make Homemade Soups 13
Chapter Two: Authentic Soup Recipes 17
French Onion Gratinee 17
French Tomato Soup 22
Jamaican Tortilla Soup 25
Jamaican Beef Soup 28
Italian Beef Veggie Soup 32
Italian Vegetable Ravioli Soup 35
Thai Coconut Soup 38
Thai Curry Soup 41
Chinese Shrimp Soup 44
Asian Chicken Noodle Soup 47
Chapter Three: Delicious Vegetarian and Vegan Soups 50
Veggie Kale Soup 50
Veggie Bean Soup 53
Vegetable Minestrone Soup 56
Lentil Soup 59
Cabbage Soup 62

Miso Soup 65
Vegan Tomato Rice Soup 67
Vegan Peanut Squash Soup 69
Butternut Squash Soup 72
Cantaloupe Soup 75
Chapter Four: Tasty Southern Soups 77
Southern Mushroom Soup 77
Southern Potato Soup 81
Southern Bean Soup 84
Southern Spaghetti Soup 87
Southern Chowder Soup 90
Southern Chicken and Rice Soup 93
Southwestern Chicken Soup 96
Southern Vegetable Soup 99
Southern Hamburger Soup 102
Deep Southern Loaded Baked Potato Soup 106

Foreword

"Slotted spoons don't hold much soup." – Stephen Sondheim

My crockpot works wonders when I decide to make a delicious soup but large pots of any kind will do just as nicely. When fall comes in and the weather starts to turn cold, soup is one of the first things humans run to for internal warmth. Even the child's lunch box of the past had a thermos that could be used either for a cold drink on a warm day or hot soup on the cold days.

Soups can be made to include a variety of meats and vegetables. The recipes included in this book are some of the most popular, the best tasting and the easiest to make. Most of them can be made in under an hour and have less than 100 calories!

If you are interested in trying soups from all around the world, look at our first chapter. There are recipes that will take you the cool French countryside, around the world to China and across the ocean to Italy. Bring overseas to your home by making these tasty soups.

Keep it healthy with our chapter on Vegetarian and Vegan recipes. These soups are some of the healthiest offered to the public. If you've already been eating a vegetarian diet, you'll know what substitutions you want to make, if there are any. You'll know what tastes good together and what you don't prefer. Try out our healthy vegan and vegetarian soup recipes till you find one you can't live without!

Our third chapter consists of ten recipes that will take you down South through your taste buds! These Southern born soups are favorites for many. We know you will find one that will make you want to visit the lower states asap!

Bonus: Your FREE Gift

As a token of our appreciation, please take advantage of the **FREE Gift** - a lifetime **VIP Membership** at our book club.

Follow the link below to download your FREE books:

http://bit.ly/vipbookclub

As a VIP member, you will get an instant **FREE** access to exclusive new releases and bestselling books.

Chapter One: Why You Should Make Homemade Soups

"Anyone who tells a lie has not pure heart, and cannot make good soup." – Ludwig Von Beethoven

In this chapter, I will help you to:

- Understand why homemade soups are an excellent choice

- Get some tips that will make your soup making superb

Why should you make homemade soup?

A better question might be why shouldn't you start making homemade soups. As soon as the cooler weather kicks in, it is natural to start looking at what soups are available when you're on your lunch break or coming home from work. You can buy lots of soups in the can. In fact, there are many varieties and brands that are inexpensive and tasty.

But why not take control of what your soups contain? Have you looked at the list of ingredients in your canned soups? It certainly has a lot more ingredients than "meat and vegetables, broth and seasonings". There might be a few ingredients you can't pronounce.

Making your own soups is the best way to know exactly what's going in your food. You know there aren't any foreign elements of any kind. Whether you are using frozen vegetables or fresh, chicken, pork or beef, you are in control.

Try making just one recipe and see if you don't get in the habit of trying your hand at making homemade soups of all kinds.

Tips to Making the Best Soup

Do you sometimes wonder how your aunt, mother or grandmother got her soup to taste so wonderfully delicious? Or perhaps you didn't have the opportunity to have a relative preparing homemade soups for everyone in the family and you think it's about time someone did.

Whether you've been cooking for a long time or you've just started, the recipes we've provided are clear and concise enough for anyone to make. Here are some quick tips to help you get started on your soup-making venture:

1. Focus on the quality of the broth. If you are just using water, add a bouillon cube for extra flavoring, make a broth from cheese or put together a vegetable broth in just a few minutes. A good broth can either make or break the soup you're trying to make.

2. Make sure you are adding one or two vegetables to your soup, even if you don't plan to eat them. Celery is one of the most common vegetables to be added to a soup to give it a certain flavor, while the celery is not itself eaten. The same can be said for bay leaves, which should always be removed before serving.

3. Some of the best vegetables that can be used for soups is potatoes, beets, carrots, turnips, cabbage, broccoli, mushrooms and celery, as well as green beans and peas. Leafy greens are a great addition and include types such as spinach and kale. Both leafy greens are an acquired taste so use only what is given in the recipe instructions or even try it to taste.

4. Understand your vegetables. Know how long it takes to cook each one. Some are harder in form than others and may take longer, such as potatoes and carrots. Celery and onions will take much less time cooking than the harder formed veggies. Get to know how long

it takes to cook each one so you will know when to add them and will adjust your recipe to your desired vegetable consistency.

Chapter Two: Authentic Soup Recipes

"If a cook can't make soup between two and seven, she can't make it in a week." – Anthony Trollop

In this chapter, you will learn:

- Ten recipes to try featuring authentic tastes
- Tips to making your soup just right

French Onion Gratinee

Prep Time	15 min
Cook Time	1 hour

Total Time	1 hour 15 min
Serving Size	4
Calories	74
Carbs	22.3g

Ingredients

- 4 tbsp. butter
- 1 tsp salt
- 14oz can of beef broth
- 1 tbsp. Worcestershire sauce
- 48oz can of chicken broth
- 3 medium sweet onions, sliced thin
- 2 medium red onion, sliced thin

- ½ c red wine

- Salt and pepper

- 1 bay leaf

- 1 ½ tbsp. balsamic vinegar

- 4 thick slices of French bread

- 8 slices of Swiss cheese, warm

- ½ c shredded Asiago cheese, warm

- 4 pinches of paprika

Let's Cook:

1. Melt the butter over medium heat in a large pot. Add all onions and some salt. Cook for 35 minutes, stirring occasionally. Onions should be caramelized to a syrupy consistency.

2. Mix in the beef and chicken broth, red wine and Worcestershire sauce. Bundle the thyme, bay leaf and parsley together with twine and put it in the pot. Simmer for 20 minutes over medium heat.

3. Remove the herbs and discard them.

4. Reduce heat to low, season with pepper and salt and mix in the vinegar. Cover. Keep it warm over a low heat as you prepare the bread.

5. Preheat the broiler of your oven. Arrange the bread on a baking sheet. Broil for 90 seconds, turn over and broil another 90 seconds. Bread should be well toasted on both sides. Take out the bread but leave your broiler on.

6. Put four oven safe bowls on a rimmed baking sheet. Each bowl should be filled 2/3 with hot soup and place a piece of bread on top of each, 2 slices of swiss and ¼ of the Asiago. Sprinkle with paprika and broil for 5 minutes.

7. Serve immediately after removing from oven.

Extra Tip:

You can use aluminum foil when baking to make the clean-up much easier.

French Tomato Soup

Prep Time	20 mins
Cook Time	1 hour 15 mins
Total Time	1 hours 35 mins
Serving Size	4
Calories	65
Carbs	12.4g

Ingredients:

- 1 tbsp. butter
- 6 chopped tomatoes
- 1 lg potato, peeled and chopped
- 6 c chicken broth

- 1 lg onion

- 1 pressed garlic clove

- 1 bay leaf

- ½ c long grain rice

- 1 tsp salt

Let's Cook:

1. Melt the butter in a saucepan over medium heat. Add onions and sauté for ten minutes until lightly browned. Onions should be tender.

2. Add tomatoes. Cook for ten minutes, stirring often.

3. Add potato and two cups of chicken broth. Season with garlic, bay leaf and salt. Bring the mixture to a boil. Reduce heat and simmer for about 20 minutes, covered.

4. Stir in the rest of the chicken broth and heat it to a boil again. Take out the bay leaf and strain the solid matter from the broth. Place both to the side.

5. Puree the veggies in a blender or processor and add them back to the broth, stirring well.

6. Once the mix is boiling, add the rice. Cover.

7. Simmer for 15 minutes over a low heat. Rice should be tender.

8. Serve.

Jamaican Tortilla Soup

Prep Time	20 mins
Cook Time	20 mins
Total Time	40 mins
Serving Size	4
Calories	95.8
Carbs	39.2g

Ingredients

- 8 tsp chicken bouillon
- ¼ tsp ground allspice
- ½ tsp chopped thyme (fresh is preferred for better taste)
- 1 c chopped carrots

- 3 boneless, skinless chicken breasts, cut in half
- 1/8 tsp ground cinnamon
- 1 tbsp. minced garlic
- 1 tbsp. chopped ginger
- 1 c chopped tomato
- 1 tsp hot pepper sauce
- 1 c coconut milk
- 1 c shredded mozzarella
- 2 c crispy tortilla strips
- 2 wedged limes

Let's Cook:

1. Preheat an indoor and outdoor grill over a medium heat. Grill chicken breasts for 8 minutes each. They should be brown and cooked through. Remove from the grill. Cut the chicken into chunks.

2. Combine the chicken, bouillon, carrots and water in a large pot. Season with thyme, cinnamon, garlic, ginger and allspice.

3. Bring to a boil and then reduce to a low heat to simmer for 10 minutes over a medium heat. Carrots should be tender. Pour in the coconut milk, hot pepper sauce and tomato. Heat all the way through but do not bring it to a boil.

4. Ladle the soup into bowls and then top it with mozzarella and tortilla strips. Squeeze the juice from the limes onto the soup and serve.

Extra Tip:

Flour tortilla strips are preferred for this recipe, as corn strips will create a different taste. However, if you personally prefer corn, they will suffice.

Jamaican Beef Soup

Prep Time	20 mins
Cook Time	15 mins
Total Time	35 mins
Serving Size	4
Calories	89
Carbs	91.2g

Ingredients

- 2 lbs. stewing beef
- 8 c water
- 2 chopped carrots
- 3 c butternut squash, diced

- 1 peels and sliced chayote (have 16 pieces)
- 1 c diced turnip
- 1 lb. peeled, cubed yellow yam
- 3 chopped stalks of celery
- 1 chopped lg onion
- 1 pkg Jamaican beef-pumpkin soup mix
- ½ chopped red and green bell pepper
- 1 pkg chicken soup mix or a can of chicken soup
- ¼ tsp black pepper
- Scotch Bonnet Pepper to taste
- 2 sprigs fresh thyme
- 1 tbsp. butter

For the Dumplings:

- 1/3 c water

- 1 c flour

- ½ tsp salt

Mix together to make the dough stiff. Form into 8 round, flat dumplings.

Let's Cook:

1. Bring the water to a boil. Add diced butternut squash and beef.

2. Cover the pot and lower the heat to medium-low. Cook for 1 hour. Squash should be dissolved. Beef should be tender.

3. Add in the chayote, turnip, carrots and celery. Cook for one hour. Beef should be tender.

4. Add the dumplings and yam to the pot. Boil for 15 minutes.

5. Add onions, bell peppers and chicken soup to the pot.

6. Add the thyme, pepper and butter. Stir well.

7. Put the bonnet pepper on the top of the soup, cover and cook over a rolling boil for five minutes. Take out the bonnet pepper and the thyme.

8. Turn off your stove and serve right away.

Italian Beef Veggie Soup

Prep Time	10 mins
Cook Time	20 mins
Total Time	30 mins
Serving Size	4
Calories	72
Carbs	12.9g

Ingredients

- 1 onion
- 1 head of broccoli
- 1 head of cauliflower
- 1 c fresh mushrooms

- 4 carrots

- 1 lb. beef stew meat

- 1 oz. beef base

- 2 cans of Italian tomato paste

- ½ gallon of water

- 1 can of Italian stewed tomatoes

Let's Cook:

1. Chop up the onion and add it to a large kettle with the meat. Brown the meat and add ½ gallon of water in the kettle. Add the beef base.

2. Cut up the vegetables. Add to the kettle with tomato paste, stewed tomatoes and Italian seasonings.

3. Let the mixture simmer until vegetables are tender. Mix well and serve.

Extra Tip:

Italian Vegetable Ravioli Soup

Prep Time	25 mins
Cook Time	25 mins
Total Time	50 mins
Serving Size	2 cups
Calories	261
Carbs	33 g

Ingredients

- 1 tbsp. extra-virgin olive oil
- 2 minced cloves of garlic
- 2 c thawed and diced frozen bell pepper and onion mix
- 15oz can of reduced-sodium chicken broth

- ¼ tsp crushed red pepper
- 28oz can of crushed tomatoes
- 1 ½ c hot water
- 9oz pkg fresh meat ravioli
- Fresh ground pepper to taste
- 2 c medium diced zucchini
- 1 tsp dried basil

Let's Cook:

1. Heat up oil in the large pot. Add pepper-onion mix, crushed red pepper and garlic. Cook for one minute, stirring. Add water, broth, basil and tomatoes.

2. Bring to a rolling boil over high. Add your ravioli and cook for three minutes. Add the zucchini. Bring it to a boil. Cook the zucchini until it is crisp and tender. Season with the pepper.

Thai Coconut Soup

Prep Time	35 mins
Cook Time	30 mins
Total Time	1 hour 5 mins
Serving Size	6
Calories	135
Carbs	29.2g

Ingredients

- 1 tbsp. olive oil
- 4 c chicken broth
- 2 tbsps. grated fresh ginger
- 2 tsp. red curry paste

- 3 tbsp. fish sauce

- 1 tbsp. light brown sugar

- 3 cans of coconut milk

- ½ lb. sliced fresh shiitake mushrooms

- 2 tbsps. fresh lime juice

- Salt to taste

- 1/3 c chopped fresh cilantro

- 1 lb. med. peeled and deveined shrimp

Let's Cook:

1. Heat olive oil over medium heat in a large pot. Add in curry paste and ginger. Stir and cook for one minute. Pour the chicken broth over the mixture slowly, stirring the whole time.

2. Stir in the brown sugar and fish sauce. Simmer for about 15 minutes.

3. Stir in mushrooms and coconut milk. Cook while stirring until the mushrooms are tender. This should take 5 minutes.

4. Add in the shrimp and cook until they are no longer translucent. This should be another 5 minutes.

5. Add the lime juice and season with the salt.

6. Garnish with cilantro and serve.

Extra Tip:

Chop up your veggies into smaller bites to reduce cooking time. If you use this method, however, always keep in mind how long it takes to cook through certain vegetables, so that you know which vegetables needs to be added at what time.

Thai Curry Soup

Prep Time	15 mins
Cook Time	35 mins
Total Time	50 mins
Serving Size	6
Calories	109
Carbs	31g

Ingredients

- 1 tbsp. olive oil
- 1 minced garlic clove
- 1 tsp ground ginger
- 2 oz. rice noodles

- 2 tsp. red curry paste
- 32 oz. chicken broth
- 1 tbsp. white sugar
- 2 tbsp. soy sauce
- 13.5 oz. can of reduced-fat coconut milk
- ½ c deveined, peeled medium shrimp
- 10 oz. bag baby spinach leaves
- ½ c sliced mushrooms
- 2 tbsp. fresh lime juice
- 2 thin sliced green onions
- 1/3 c chopped cilantro

Let's Cook:

1. Bring some salted water in a pot to a boil. Then add rice noodles. Cook for 3 minutes. Drain and rinse well, using cold water. Set it aside.

2. Heat up your oil over a medium heat in a large pot. Stir in the ginger and garlic. Cook for 60 seconds. Add some curry paste and cook for another 30 seconds.

3. Pour in ½ c of chicken broth. Stir until the paste has dissolved. Pour the rest of the chicken stock into the pot with the rest of the sugar and soy sauce. Bring it to a boil. Reduce heat to medium-low and partially cover. Simmer for 20 minutes.

4. Stir in the coconut milk, mushrooms, lime juice, spinach, shrimp and cilantro. Increase to medium high heat. Simmer until the shrimp become pink for 5 minutes.

5. Place rice noodles into each serving bowl. Ladle the soup on top and serve with a garnish of sliced green onions sprinkled on top.

Chinese Shrimp Soup

Prep Time	5 mins
Cook Time	7 mins
Total Time	12 mins
Serving Size	4
Calories	97
Carbs	22.3g

Ingredients

- 4 c chicken stock
- 6 oz. Chinese noodles (whichever you prefer)
- 1 tbsp. low sodium dark soy sauce
- Lime juice

- 1-star anise

- 20 raw deveined, cleaned shrimp

- 1 chopped small head of Bok Choy

- 1 tbsp. brown sugar

- 1 tbsp. fish sauce

- 1 tbsp. light soy sauce

- 3 green onions

- Chili flakes

Let's Cook:

1. Noodles should be cooked per the pkg instructions.

2. Drain.

3. Add fish sauce, lime juice, brown sugar, bok choy, green onions, soy sauces and chicken stock to a large pot.

4. Bring the mix to a boil and add the shrimp. Cook until the shrimp is pink. Add noodles.

5. Warm the mixture thoroughly. Pour into a bowl and top with chili flakes.

Asian Chicken Noodle Soup

Prep Time	15 mins
Cook Time	7 mins
Total Time	22 mins
Serving Size	6
Calories	184
Carbs	21 g

Ingredients

- 2 tbsp. mirin
- 4 tbsp. soy sauce
- 2 tsp dark sesame oil
- 1 minced garlic clove

- 1 tbsp. sugar
- 2 tbsp. minced fresh ginger
- 4 tbsp. rice vinegar
- 8 c chicken broth
- ½ tsp Vietnamese chile paste
- 4 c chopped Chinese vegetables
- 12 oz. skinless, boneless, thin sliced chicken breast
- 1 pkg rice noodles
- 6 scallions thin-sliced
- ½ c fresh cilantro leaves, chopped

Let's Cook:

1. In a small mixing bowl, stir together mirin, soy sauce, garlic, sugar, vinegar, 1 tsp of sesame oil and vinegar.

2. Heat up the broth in a medium saucepan, stirring occasionally for five minutes. Add in the mixture you just made, the chicken and the vegetables. Bring the mix to a boil. Lower the heat and simmer for 2 minutes. Chicken should be cooked through. Add the other tsp of sesame oil. Adjust the seasonings to your taste.

3. Pour the mix over the prepared Chinese noodles.

4. Garnish with the scallions and cilantro.

Chapter Three: Delicious Vegetarian and Vegan Soups

"Alphabet soup is my magic eight ball. Served hot or cold, words are delicious." – Amanda Mosher

In this chapter, you'll receive:

- 10 delicious Vegan and Vegetarian recipes
- Tips for several delicious soup recipes

Veggie Kale Soup

Prep Time	25 mins
Cook Time	30 mins

Total Time	55 mins
Serving Size	4
Calories	77
Carbs	14.3g

Ingredients

- 1 yellow onion
- 2 tbsps. olive oil
- 2 tbsp. chopped garlic
- 1 bunch kale with the stems removed and chopped leaves
- 8 c water
- 6 peeled and cubed white potatoes
- 2 drained cans of cannellini beans

- 1 tbsp. Italian seasoning
- 2 tbsps. dried parsley
- Salt and pepper to taste
- 1 can of diced tomatoes

Let's Cook:

1. In a large pot, heat the olive oil. Add garlic and onions until they are soft. Stir in the kale. Cook for two minutes until wilted.

2. Stir in vegetable bouillon, water, potatoes, beans, parsley, Italian seasoning and tomatoes.

3. Simmer for 25 minutes over medium heat. Potatoes should be cooked through.

4. Season with salt and pepper. Serve immediately while hot.

Veggie Bean Soup

Prep Time	5 mins
Cook Time	10 mins
Total Time	15 mins
Serving Size	4
Calories	213
Carbs	32.9

Ingredients

- 2 cans 15oz cans of black beans, do not drain
- ½ c salsa
- 1 tbsp. chili powder
- 16oz can of vegetable broth

- Sour cream, shredded cheese, chopped onion and chopped cilantro optional for toppings

Let's Cook:

1. Put one can of the beans into a food processor with a bit of water to process until they are almost smooth.

2. Pour both cans into a saucepan. Add in salsa, chili powder and vegetable broth. Bring to a boil.

3. Heat over medium heat until hot. Serve with toppings of choice.

Extra Tip:

Always let your soup cool off a bit before you taste-test it. You will scald your tongue and you won't get a proper flavor test. Over seasoning happens easily when you can judge the flavor with a scalded tongue.

Vegetable Minestrone Soup

Prep Time	10 mins
Cook Time	80 mins
Total Time	90 mins
Serving Size	4
Calories	84
Carbs	13.5g

Ingredients

- 4 c diced tomatoes
- ½ tsp oregano
- 4 c vegetable broth
- 1 tbsp. fresh basil chopped

- 2 chopped carrots
- ½ chopped onion
- 1 c chopped green beans
- 3 chopped zucchinis
- 3 minced cloves of garlic
- 1 bay leaf
- Pepper and salt to taste

Let's Cook:

1. In a large pot, add vegetable broth, basil, carrots, diced tomatoes, oregano, celery, zucchini, garlic, green beans, onion and bay leaf.

2. Slowly bring the soup to a simmer on low. Allow it to cook for an hour. Vegetables should be tender.

3. Add macaroni pasta, salt and pepper and bring up the heat to medium low. Allow it to simmer for 20 minutes until pasta is done cooking.

Extra Tip:

For maximum creaminess in your soups, try using a can of coconut milk as opposed to non-dairy unsweetened milk. Try adding a handful of cashews to the coconut milk and blend until it creates a delicious nutritious cream.

Lentil Soup

Prep Time	5 mins
Cook Time	50 mins
Total Time	55 mins
Serving Size	4
Calories	230
Carbs	33g

Ingredients

- 1 diced onion
- 1 sliced carrot
- 1 tsp olive oil
- 1 c dry brown lentils

- 4 c vegetable broth
- 2 bay leaves
- ¼ tsp dried thyme
- Salt and pepper to taste

Let's Cook:

1. Sauté onions and carrot in a large pot with vegetable oil for 5 minutes. Onion should be clear.

2. Add the lentils, thyme, vegetable broth and salt and pepper to taste.

3. Reduce the heat to simmer and cover. Cook for 45 minutes until lentils are soft.

4. Remove the bay leaves and serve with preferred garnish.

Cabbage Soup

Prep Time	10 mins
Cook Time	20 mins
Total Time	30 mins
Serving Size	6
Calories	72
Carbs	12.8

Ingredients

- 2 chopped onions
- 2 c vegetable broth
- 2 minced garlic cloves
- 1 lb. chopped cabbage

- Salt and pepper

- Hot sauce to taste

- Chopped cilantro for garnish

Let's Cook:

1. Mix together all your ingredients (except cilantro) in a large saucepan. Simmer for 20 minutes covered, stirring occasionally, over medium-high heat.

2. Transfer to a processor and blend until it is smooth.

3. Reheat in the saucepan and stir in the fresh cilantro just before you serve it. Add hot sauce, salt and pepper to taste for added seasoning if needed.

Extra Tip:

A pinch of salt will help season your soup. You can also use bouillon cubes as a form of seasoning, especially if you have used water as the liquid in your soup instead of broth.

Miso Soup

Prep Time	5 mins
Cook Time	10 mins
Total Time	15 mins
Serving Size	6
Calories	91
Carbs	8.6g

Ingredients

- 4 c water
- ½ c miso
- 1 tbsp. shredded wakame seaweed
- 3 chopped scallions

- ½ tsp sesame oil

- ½ block silken tofu cut into 1 inch cubes

- Dash of soy sauce

Let's Cook:

1. In a large pot, bring water to a simmer and add seaweed. Allow it to simmer for 6 minutes. Keep in mind you will have less salty fishy flavor the longer you let it simmer.

2. Reduce the heat to the minimum and add all other ingredients. Stir until the miso is dissolved. Do not boil. It will ruin the healthy properties and change the flavor.

3. Serve with a smile.

Vegan Tomato Rice Soup

Prep Time	2 mins
Cook Time	15 mins
Total Time	17 mins
Serving Size	6
Calories	112
Carbs	11.2g

Ingredients

- 2 tbsp. flour
- 1 tbsp. vegetable oil
- 1 diced onion
- 4 c canned tomato sauce

- 2 c cooked leftover rice

Let's Cook:

1. Heat up the oil in a saucepan. Brown the flour in oil.

2. Add the onion and tomato sauce.

3. Cook for 15 minutes over low heat.

4. Add rice and cook until the soup is cooked through.

Vegan Peanut Squash Soup

Prep Time	15 mins
Cook Time	50 mins
Total Time	1 hour 5 mins
Serving Size	6
Calories	189
Carbs	20.1g

Ingredients

- 2 tbsp. peanut oil
- 1 c brown rice
- 1 tbsp. grated fresh ginger
- 2 finely chopped yellow onions

- 3 finely chopped garlic cloves
- 1 finely chopped small green serrano chili
- 1 tsp ground cumin
- 4 c vegetable broth
- 2 tsp kosher salt
- 2 tbsp. peanut oil
- ½ c smooth peanut butter
- 2 tbsp. brown sugar
- 1 shredded cooked chicken breast
- 2 tbsp. chopped roasted peanuts
- 2 16oz cans of rinsed black eyed peas
- 28oz can of tomato puree
- 1 medium peeled, seeded acorn squash cut into 1-inch chunks

Let's Cook:

1. Heat oil over medium heat in a skillet. Add onions and cook for 15 minutes. Add cumin, salt, chili, garlic and ginger. Cook another 5 minutes, stirring often.

2. Add in tomato puree, broth, acorn squash, sugar and peanut butter.

3. Cook for 30 minutes over medium heat, covered. Squash should be tender.

4. Add in peas and heat all the way through. Split the soup in half and add the chicken to one-half. Sprinkle with the peanuts and serve with rice.

Extra Tip:

Make large batches of your soup and freeze them for future use. Allow your frozen soup to thaw in the fridge or place it in a soup pot and put the heat on low.

Butternut Squash Soup

Prep Time	25 mins
Cook Time	15 mins
Total Time	40 mins
Serving Size	6
Calories	222
Carbs	44g

Ingredients

- 1 bay leaf
- 5 c low-sodium vegetable broth
- 1 3lb peeled butternut squash, cut into 1-inch chunks
- 4 chopped leeks

- Salt and black pepper
- 1 sliced baguette
- 2 tsp olive oil
- ¼ roughly chopped shelled raw pumpkin seeds
- 1 tbsp. roughly chopped fresh rosemary

Let's Cook:

1. In a large saucepan, put together the leeks, bay leaf, broth, squash, ¾ tsp salt and ¼ tsp pepper. Bring this mix to a boil.

2. Reduce heat to low and simmer for about 10 minutes until the squash is tender, stirring occasionally.

3. Remove the bay leaf and discard. Puree the soup until smooth using your blender, working in batches.

4. Heat the oil over medium heat in a skillet. Add in seeds and rosemary. Heat for 3 minutes, stirring occasionally.

5. Put the soup in bowls and sprinkle with rosemary mixture.

6. Serve with bread.

Cantaloupe Soup

Prep Time	10 mins
Cook Time	10 mins
Total Time	20 mins
Serving Size	6
Calories	81
Carbs	19g

Ingredients

- 1 lg seeded, chilled cantaloupe, cut up into 1-inch chunks
- 4 lime wedges
- ½ c orange juice

Let's Cook:

1. Put the cantaloupe in a blender.

2. Add orange juice and puree until well blended.

3. Divide the soup into four servings. Squeeze the limes over the soup.

4. Serve chilled.

Extra Tip:

Know your vegetables. Garlic, celery, carrots and onions are aromatics that will make your soup smell delicious. When you use them, cook them until they are soft. This is when they will release their flavor.

Chapter Four: Tasty Southern Soups

"If it was raining soup, you'd be out there with a fork." – Robin Hobb

In this chapter, I'll help you to:

- Go down South with your taste buds
- Delight your family with these Southern delicacies on a cold day

Southern Mushroom Soup

Prep Time	10 mins

Cook Time	20 mins
Total Time	30 mins
Serving Size	6
Calories	118
Carbs	20.1g

Ingredients

- 1 small chopped onion
- 2 c chopped fresh mushrooms
- 3 tbsp. melted butter
- 3 tbsp. all-purpose flour
- 1 ½ c milk
- ½ c heavy cream

- 2 c chicken broth

- Pinch of salt and pepper

- 4 slices toasted white bread

- 1 c shredded sharp Cheddar

- 1 tbsp. softened butter

Let's Cook:

1. Combine onion, chicken broth and mushrooms in a large saucepan. Bring the mixture to a boil and simmer for 15 minutes while covered over a low heat.

2. Stir melted butter and flour together in a small bowl to make a paste. Mix this in with the vegetables. Raise the heat to medium and add the milk in gradually, stirring constantly.

3. Keep stirring until the mixture thickens. It should be boiling when you stir in the cream.

4. Cook over a low heat for ten minutes. Mushrooms should be tender. Season with pepper and salt.

5. Spoon out the soup into four bowls and trim pieces of toast to fit each. Make sure the toast is buttered and place each piece on the bowls of soup. Sprinkle cheese over the bread and serve right away for the best taste.

Extra Tip:

Be careful when you boil your soup. Reduce boiling soup to a simmer and leave it there for the best taste. If you let your soup boil for too long, your vegetables will be mushy and nearly dissolve, the meat will toughen and if you are using noodles, they will break down.

Southern Potato Soup

Prep Time	15 mins
Cook Time	30 mins
Total Time	45 mins
Serving Size	6
Calories	75
Carbs	19.8g

Ingredients

- 5 washed, cubed and peeled russet potatoes
- 4 c chicken broth
- 1 c instant potato flakes
- 1 c cheddar cheese

- 1 diced onion

- 1 c whipping cream

- 1 c smoked chopped ham

- Salt and pepper to taste

Let's Cook:

1. Pour the broth into your soup pot. Place over medium heat.

2. Chop up your onion and peeled potatoes. Add broth and ham. Season with pepper and salt to taste.

3. Bring the soup to a boil. Reduce the heat and cover for fifteen minutes to simmer until potatoes are tender.

4. Take off the lid and stir in the potato flakes. Add the cream and cheese. Cook until heated thoroughly, stirring the whole time.

5. Taste and add any seasonings you need. Serve right away, adding your favorite toppings.

Southern Bean Soup

Prep Time	20 mins
Cook Time	1 hour
Total Time	1 hour 20 mins
Serving Size	4
Calories	98
Carbs	15.6g

Ingredients

- 4 cans of undrained Navy beans
- 2 chopped stalks of celery
- 1 tsp minced garlic
- 2-4 ham hocks

- 1 chopped onion
- 4 bouillon cubes
- 1 c instant mashed potato flakes
- 1 tsp salt
- 1 tsp pepper
- ½ c butter (one stick)

Let's Cook:

1. Put six cups of water in your soup pot with the bouillon cubes. Add in the ham and bring to a boil, covered.

2. Reduce the heat and simmer for 30 minutes.

3. Put the butter in a large skillet and melt over medium heat. Add celery, garlic and onion. Sauté until lightly brown.

4. Take the ham hocks out of the broth and let them cool. Dice them up and set aside.

5. Add potato flakes to the broth and stir. Add the beans, ham and onion mixture. Season with salt and pepper to taste. Bring the soup to a boil while stirring the whole time. Reduce the heat when you see it rolling and simmer for 30 minutes.

6. Serve and enjoy!

Southern Spaghetti Soup

Prep Time	15 mins
Cook Time	25 mins
Total Time	40 mins
Serving Size	4
Calories	81
Carbs	22.1g

Ingredients

- 2 cans diced tomatoes
- 1 stalk of celery
- 2 carrots
- 1 c spaghetti sauce

- 2 cans kidney beans

- 2 c water

- Handful of spaghetti noodles

- 1 tbsp. Italian seasoning

Let's Cook:

1. Pour the tomatoes, water, kidney beans and sauce into a large pot. Peel and chop up the carrots, dice up the celery and add them all to the pot. Add seasoning.

2. Bring the mix to a boil and reduce the heat. Simmer for about ten minutes. Vegetables should be tender.

3. Add noodles after breaking them into one-inch pieces. Continue with your cooking until the pasta is tender.

4. Serve with garlic toast if you like.

Southern Chowder Soup

Prep Time	15 mins
Cook Time	37 mins
Total Time	52 mins
Serving Size	6
Calories	223
Carbs	28.5g

Ingredients

- 2 tbsp. margarine
- 1 seeded and chopped jalapeno pepper
- 1 chopped medium onion
- ½ tsp paprika

- 2 cubed large red potatoes
- 1 tsp salt
- 14.5 oz. can of chicken broth
- 3 c milk
- 3 c frozen corn
- 1 chopped medium green bell pepper
- 2 tsp Dijon mustard
- 4 green onions
- ½ c flour
- ½ tsp crushed red pepper flakes

Let's Cook

1. Sauté the pepper and onion in a large saucepan until they are tender. Add the potatoes and broth. Bring this to a boil.

2. Reduce the heat and let it simmer for fifteen minutes covered.

3. Stir in paprika, red pepper flakes, salt, jalapeno and mustard. Blend well.

4. Add green onion, 2 ½ c milk and corn. Bring it all to a boil.

5. Separately, use a medium mixing bowl to combine half a cup of milk and flour. Gradually add this mix to your chowder.

6. Bring to a boil, stirring the entire time, for two minutes. The soup should be bubbly and thick.

Southern Chicken and Rice Soup

Prep Time	25 mins
Cook Time	2 hour 30 mins
Total Time	2 hours 55 mins
Serving Size	10
Calories	218
Carbs	27g

Ingredients

- ½ tsp Creole seasoning
- 1 tsp seasoned salt
- 1 minced garlic clove
- 1 tbsp. chopped green chiles

- 3 lbs. chicken
- 2 tsp salt
- 10 c water
- ½ c chopped celery
- ½ c chopped onion
- ½ c uncooked long grain rice
- ½ c thinly sliced carrots
- ½ c frozen okra
- 1 can stewed tomatoes

Let's Cook:

1. Place your chicken, salt and water in a large soup pot or Dutch oven. Bring it to a boil.

2. Skim off the foam and reduce the heat. Cover and simmer for 60 minutes, checking at 45. Chicken should be tender.

3. Remove the chicken and set it to the side. Strip off the meat and discard the bones and skin. Cut up the chicken into bite-sized pieces.

4. Skim out the fat from the broth. Add the vegetables, seasonings and rice.

5. Leave it uncovered and cook for 30 minutes over a medium heat.

6. Put the chicken in the soup and simmer for another 30 minutes. Vegetables should be soft and tender.

Extra Tip:

Instead of Creole seasoning for this recipe, you can try substituting it with a mixture of ½ tsp garlic powder, ½ tsp paprika, ¼ tsp salt and a pinch of ground cumin, cayenne pepper and dried thyme.

Southwestern Chicken Soup

Prep Time	10 mins
Cook Time	25 mins
Total Time	35 mins
Serving Size	4
Calories	230
Carbs	24.2g

Ingredients

- ½ lb. skinless, boneless cubed chicken breast
- 2 minced garlic cloves
- ¼ c finely chopped onion
- 2 tbsp. olive oil

- 1 can of rinsed, drained black beans (15 oz.)
- 1 can chicken broth (14.5 oz.)
- 1 can drained whole kernel corn (15.25 oz.)
- 1 can undrained diced tomatoes and green chiles (10 oz.)
- 1 tsp ground cumin
- ½ tsp chili powder
- ½ tsp salt
- 1/8 tsp cayenne pepper
- Plain yogurt
- Minced cilantro

Let's Cook:

1. Heat up olive oil over medium heat in a large skillet. Add onion and chicken. Cook the mix until the chicken is not pink. This should take about 6 minutes. Add garlic and cook for another minute.

2. Stir in the corn, tomatoes, broth and seasonings. Bring the mixture to a boil.

3. Reduce the heat, simmer for 10 minutes to 15 minutes. Top each serving with cilantro and yogurt.

Southern Vegetable Soup

Prep Time	10 mins
Cook Time	20 mins
Total Time	30 mins
Serving Size	6
Calories	109
Carbs	16g

Ingredients

- 2 tsp olive oil
- 2 cans vegetable broth
- 1 pkg frozen mixed vegetables
- 1 can chopped green chiles

- 1 tsp sugar
- ½ tsp salt
- 1/8 tsp white pepper
- 3 tsp minced garlic
- ½ c chopped yellow onion
- 2 cans vegetable broth
- 1 can crushed tomatoes
- 1 c sliced fresh okra

Let's Cook:

1. In a large pot, sauté the onion in the olive oil for three minutes. The onion should be tender and soft. Add garlic and cook for one minute.

2. Stir in the rest of the ingredients. Bring to a boil.

3. Reduce the heat and cover. Simmer for 20 minutes until the vegetables are crispy but also tender.

4. Serve the soup immediately or freeze for later use.

Extra Tip:

This soup may be frozen for up to 3 months. When you plan to use it, thaw the soup in the fridge overnight. Put it in a saucepan, cover and cook until thoroughly heated through.

Southern Hamburger Soup

Prep Time	20 mins
Cook Time	1 hour 15 mins
Total Time	1 hour 35 mins
Serving Size	6
Calories	189
Carbs	18.3g

Ingredients

- 1 tbsp. cooking oil
- 1 ½ c chopped onion
- 1 tbsp. minced garlic
- 2 cans of stewed tomatoes

- ½ tsp cayenne pepper
- 1 tsp dried basil
- 4 c water
- 4 tsp beef base
- 4 c of mixed vegetables
- 1 c chopped carrots
- ¼ c chopped celery
- 1 ¼ lb. ground beef
- 1 tsp kosher salt
- ½ tsp black pepper
- 1 tsp dried oregano
- 4 c beef broth
- ½ tbsp. Worcestershire sauce
- Egg noodles

- Dried parsley

Let's Cook:

1. Sauté your onion, carrots, garlic and celery in a large soup pot. Use oil over medium heat until all the veggies are soft and tender. Add ground beef to the mix and cook all the way through.

2. Dry off excess fat.

3. Add tomatoes, juice, peppers, oregano, basil and salt. Cook over medium heat, stirring it all together over a medium heat. Stir for about 5 minutes. Add beef base, water, stock and Worcestershire sauce.

4. Increase the heat to high and bring it to a boil. When it is rolling, reduce the heat and let the soup simmer until the veggies are cooked through.

5. Taste it to make sure it is seasoned how you like it. Adjust as necessary.

6. You can either serve the soup right then or let it simmer for an hour until you are ready to

eat. You can add the egg noodles if you prefer or eat them separately.

7. When you ladle the soup out, sprinkle it with grated Parmesan cheese for an extra delicious taste.

8. Serve with rolls or bread.

Deep Southern Loaded Baked Potato Soup

Prep Time	25 mins
Cook Time	1 hour 30 mins
Total Time	1 hour 55 mins
Serving Size	6
Calories	205
Carbs	30.1g

Ingredients

- 6 slices of chopped bacon
- 6 medium potatoes
- ½ c unsalted butter
- ½ c diced celery

- ¾ c all-purpose flour
- 1 ½ c diced onion
- 1 ½ c milk
- 1 ½ c half n half
- 2 tsp minced garlic
- 5 c chicken stock
- 2 tsp kosher salt
- 6 turns on your pepper grinder
- Hot sauce to taste
- 1/3 c sour cream
- 1 ½ c shredded sharp cedar
- 1/8 c sliced green onions
- Bacon, green onion, bacon bits and/or sour cream for garnish

Let's Cook:

1. Set your oven to 425 degrees.

2. Scrub your potatoes and stab them with a fork. Put them directly on the rack for 45 minutes. Bring the heat up to medium-high.

3. Add chicken broth gradually, stirring all the while. The mixture should be smooth. Reduce the heat to simmer and let it cook for 15 minutes. Stir occasionally.

4. Stir in salt, pepper, half and half and milk. Add hot sauce if desired and potatoes. Cook for another 15 minutes. Stir every few minutes.

5. Stir in sour cream, green onions and cheese until the cheese has melted. It should be heated through completely. Garnish the bowls you use with a pinch of cheese, crumbled bacon and green onion.

6. Serve with bread.

Extra Tip:

If you plan to freeze your soup, do not use egg noodles. Add them only after your soup has been thawed and is already back to a boil. Noodles will taste bad when reheated.

Best Practices & Common Mistakes

Do's

Use water if you have no broth

With the right seasonings or just a bouillon cube, you can make water taste perfect.

Wait on the tomatoes

Tomatoes can cause beans and some vegetables to stay crunchy. Add your tomatoes at the end of the recipe to prevent this from happening.

Garnish

Soups are made so much better with a bit of garnish. Sour cream, pesto, toasted pumpkin seeds and cheese are very popular garnishes for a bowl of piping hot soup.

Don'ts

Boil when you should simmer

Always make sure you are following the directions when the recipe calls for boiling as opposed to simmering. Boiling could cause the tasty flavor to disappear and simmering too long could make the soup thicker or thinner than you desire.

Use too much salt

It is a good idea to taste as you go along through the recipe. Seasoning must be correct if you want your soup to be the best.

Overcook the veggies

Many soups can be ruined by vegetables that are so cooked they are barely together anymore.

Conclusion

Now is the time to get into cooking hot, delicious soups for your family. Most home cooks start making soup for their families around the fall season. Whether it's that time of year or not, cool days call for a tasty soup to warm up the insides.

We know you will find a couple favorites in this book. Our tips and tricks to making better soup will help you become a soup connoisseur. Your friends and family will be amazed by the delicious tastes and you'll love the way your house smells while you're cooking!

Take our advice and start making homemade soups right away. You know what you're putting in them is real, with no additives and preservatives, plus you can take out or add in whatever you want to enhance the flavor you like best!

Don't hesitate! Start making hot, delicious homemade soup meals for your family today!

Bonus: Your FREE Gift

As a token of our appreciation, please take advantage of the **FREE Gift** - a lifetime **VIP Membership** at our book club.

Follow the link below to download your FREE books:

http://bit.ly/vipbookclub

As a VIP member, you will get an instant **FREE** access to exclusive new releases and bestselling books.

Printed in Great Britain
by Amazon